Percy Grainger
THE CUTTING OF THE HAY

orchestrated for Symphonic Band
by Brian S. Wilson
(full score)

ED 4053
First Printing: November 1998

ISBN 0-634-00309-7

G. SCHIRMER, Inc.

DISTRIBUTED BY

HAL•LEONARD®
CORPORATION
7777 W. BLUEMOUND RD. P.O. BOX 13819 MILWAUKEE, WI 53213

PREFACE

This arrangement is the end product of my dissertation, "Orchestrational Archetypes in Percy Grainger's Wind Band Music." In an attempt to understand the enigmatic style of Grainger's wind band music, I made a detailed analysis of his recurring orchestrational practices with regard to melody, countermelody, part writing and contrapuntal dynamics. I concluded that the Grainger "sound" is a function of recurring orchestrational techniques, rather than other compositional elements such as melody or harmony. This information was then used to "dish up" selected Grainger voice and piano pieces in his own idiosyncratic style. (I also arranged Grainger's "British Waterside" and "Lord Maxwell's Goodnight.")

"The Cutting of the Hay," like "Molly on the Shore" and "Irish Tune from County Derry," is based on melodies found in the *Complete Petrie Collection of Ancient Irish Music*, edited by Charles Villiers Stanford. Grainger freely arranged these tunes for piano in 1908. The original is in A minor and remains so in the band version.

—BRIAN S. WILSON

Brian S. Wilson is assistant professor of music, director of instrumental music and composer-in-residence at Hartwick College, Oneonta, New York.

British Waterside, adapted by Brian Wilson, is available for purchase, order no. 50483294

British Waterside, adapted by John Moss for young band, is available for purchase, order no. 50483121

THE CUTTING OF THE HAY

Percy Grainger

orchestrated by Brian S. Wilson

G. SCHIRMER, Inc.

DISTRIBUTED BY

HAL•LEONARD®
CORPORATION

7777 W. BLUEMOUND RD. P.O. BOX 13819 MILWAUKEE, WI 53213